well over 150 THINGS SHOULD KNOW PLYMOUTH UNIVERSITY

BY OWEN LONGHURST AND CARLY WATSON
ILLUSTRATED BY JAKE ROWLINSON

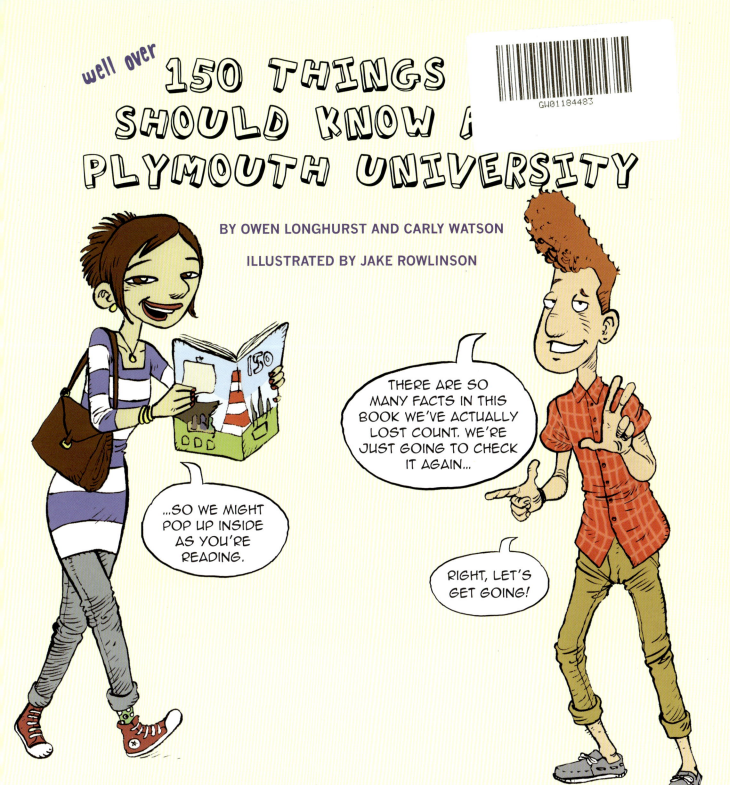

...SO WE MIGHT POP UP INSIDE AS YOU'RE READING.

THERE ARE SO MANY FACTS IN THIS BOOK WE'VE ACTUALLY LOST COUNT. WE'RE JUST GOING TO CHECK IT AGAIN...

RIGHT, LET'S GET GOING!

Did you know that Plymouth University is celebrating a very special anniversary? In 2012 higher education in Plymouth will be an incredible 150 years old! Campus life is a little different now than it was for the students of 1862. Today it isn't just about reading piles of textbooks and writing 20,000 word essays. You may not know that at this University, students have:

- built robots that can play football
- turned the campus into a mountain-bike race track
- and even held an insect film festival!

And that's just in the last decade. This book is packed with facts that will take you further back in time, to explore some of the city's history, discover some surprising things about the University – from its very beginning right through to the present day – and to dream about what the future might hold in store. So get ready; there are well over 150 facts packed inside these pages – that's at least one for every year of the University's history!

WHERE DID IT ALL BEGIN?

Six Sensational Seafarers (and one who was better at science!)

Plymouth has a proud tradition of exploration and sailing. Here are just a few interesting characters with a Plymouth connection, who have helped to inspire the city's 'Spirit of Discovery':

1) Elizabethan hero, Sir Francis Drake, was once Lord Mayor of Plymouth. He sailed from the port many times, in search of riches for his Queen.

2) In 1616, the real Pocahontas (a future Disney princess) first set foot on British soil in Plymouth.

3) The infamous pirate, Henry Avery, was born in Plymouth in the 17th century. Though he retired from piracy after just one year, it's thought he was one of the highest-earning pirates ever!

4) In 1839, speedy Edward Chaffers sailed from Plymouth to New Zealand in just 96 days – a record at the time!

5) In 1914, Ernest Shackleton's ship, *Endurance*, left Plymouth, with a plan to cross Antarctica, via the South Pole. The ship became stuck in thick ice and sank! Luckily, the crew had already escaped and were rescued... eventually.

6) In 1966, Devon-born Sir Francis Chichester sailed out of Plymouth and right around the world in a super-swift 226 days! He was the first Englishman ever to do this completely on his own.

7) Charles Darwin may have been a super scientist, but he wasn't so great at sailing. He set out from Plymouth in 1831 on the expedition that sparked his theory of evolution and was so seasick at first, that he could only eat raisins!

A Seaside City

In 1690 Plymouth had the best navy in the world and wanted to keep it that way! In order to compete with other nations, the country needed a new naval base, where ships could anchor safely for repair, and sail swiftly out to sea again at the threat of battle. The mouth of the River Tamar made a natural harbour. Nearby, the large town of Plymouth had excellent defences – the walls of the Royal Citadel were over 20 metres high! Plymouth Dock quickly became Devonport and by 1879 the Dockyard employed over 4,000 people.

The port at Plymouth stretched back even further in history, and by the 1840s Millbay Dock was growing fast. In the late 1800s a fantastic variety of cargoes arrived here, including:

- potatoes, sugar, and codfish
- cattle, paying passengers
- and even bird poo (used to fertilize crops)!

Did you know?
In 1800 Plymouth's population was just 16,000. By 1901 it had reached a whopping 107,000. In 1914, Stonehouse, Plymouth and Devonport merged to form a new city and the population soared to over 185,000!

Ships came from all corners of Europe and far-off North and South America. In 1861, over 2,000 merchant seamen were working in Plymouth.

University Challenge

There were plenty of work opportunities in Plymouth, but before 1862 the Mechanics Institute was the only place where people could learn new skills, and it was bursting at the seams.

Children would soon be expected to go to school – and stay there until they were ten years old! With more people able to read and write, more of them might dream of good training, a better job and a brighter future. So, the arrival of the School of Navigation was great news for the town – but you had to be pretty clever to get a place on a course here!

WOW! THE FEES ARE LESS THAN 30P A WEEK?

THAT'S CHEAPER THAN A CHOCOLATE BAR!

PLYMOUTH SCHOOL OF NAVIGATION IS SEARCHING FOR SAILORS OF THE FUTURE

ARE YOU a maths wizard, another Isaac Newton AND a superstar sportsman? Could you cope with the challenge of taking charge of a ship?

YES? Then WE want to hear from YOU!

WE OFFER the best ship's master and mate courses in the country, with a Certificate of Competency AND your very own copy of The Apprentice's Handbook.

FEES BETWEEN SIXPENCE AND SIX SHILLINGS PER WEEK!

NB Women and girls need not apply.

OPENING 24TH OCTOBER 1862

A School for Merchant Navy Cadets

So why a school of navigation?

"In 1835, 524 British merchant ships were stranded or wrecked, 30 ships were declared missing or lost and 564 people were drowned!"

Statistics from the Select Committee Report on the Causes of Shipwrecks, 1836

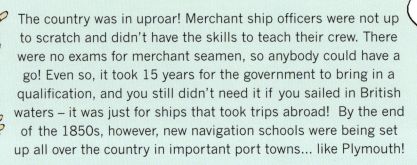

The country was in uproar! Merchant ship officers were not up to scratch and didn't have the skills to teach their crew. There were no exams for merchant seamen, so anybody could have a go! Even so, it took 15 years for the government to bring in a qualification, and you still didn't need it if you sailed in British waters – it was just for ships that took trips abroad! By the end of the 1850s, however, new navigation schools were being set up all over the country in important port towns… like Plymouth!

Student Life Past and Present

By 1871, an incredible 2,100 Merchant Officers had graduated from the School of Navigation. But the student experience wasn't completely different in the 1860s compared with today:

I want to be a Merchant Ship Captain

The 1862 Student

Name – Frederick Wilson

Age – 18

Course – Preparing for Sea - I'm at the School of Navigation for a few months, then I'm off to sea for four years! When I come back I'll carry on studying for my Certificate of Competency as a second mate.

I live – on the Barbican with my parents and 15 other people. It's a squeeze, but there's overcrowding all around the town.

Job – My parents pay my fees, but I help my father on his fishing boat whenever I can.

The 2012 Student

Name – Olivia Jones

Age – 19

Course – Marine Studies

I live – in Mary Newman Student Halls of Residence, but spend most of the holidays at sea with the shipping company that sponsors me. The company also pays for most of my tuition fees, accommodation and food!

I want 2B a Merchant Ship Captain

What, No Women?

For a whole hundred years the School of Navigation was strictly boys only. But that all changed in 1968, when Sheila Edmundson became the first female cadet from Plymouth School of Navigation to join the Merchant Navy!

Five Fun Things About Plymouth Merchant Navy Cadets

Cadets from the 1940s were expected to wear a Merchant Navy apprentice uniform with a Plymouth School of Navigation cap badge. Hair had to be really short and smart at all times. But they were allowed to have fun sometimes...

Did you know?
There were 123 day and 30 evening students enrolled at the School of Navigation in 1920.

1) Cadets had lessons on Saturday mornings – no lie-ins allowed! But on Saturday afternoons they were given time off to take part in games, sports and special events.

2) After the harsh winter of 1962, a group of cadets were awarded a special certificate for rescuing distressed farm animals from the snow-swept moors!

3) The School of Navigation had a training ship called *Tectona*. The 80-tonne whopper served the cadets for 16 years.

4) In the 1960s the school held a water-based sports day. In one exciting event, cadets raced to rescue a man from a sinking ship!

5) In 1975 Nautical Studies lecturer, Dr Ken George, brought his passion for theatre to the school, turning up to give a lecture in the full naval uniform of Captain Corcoran from the comic opera *HMS Pinafore*!

Did you know?
The School of Navigation didn't tolerate time-wasters. The Apprentice's Handbook, a rulebook given to every cadet, advised them not to be late, cause trouble, or get ideas above their station!

But not everyone who studied at Plymouth was interested in the sea – some people preferred working on dry land. Over time, plenty more courses became available.

WARTIME WOES

Between July 1940 and April 1944, over 6000 high-explosive bombs and around 200,000 fire bombs fell on Plymouth. The heaviest attacks happened over seven nights in March and April, 1941. This became known as the 'Plymouth Blitz'.

"DID YOU SEE THAT?"

The Plymouth Post

BOMB-BLITZ CATASTROPHE: PORTLAND SQUARE SHELTER SHATTERED!

23rd April 1941

At least 76 people died last night in an air-raid shelter bombing, with many more killed in other bombings around the city. Ten-year-old Arthur Davis witnessed German planes howling through the night sky and watched in horror as the Portland Square air-raid shelter took a direct hit. "The noise was horrendous," he told our reporter. "I stood there staring, I couldn't believe it was happening."

HEROIC HOUND!

Lillian Saunders heard reports on the wireless that bombs would fall on Plymouth. "I gathered my things quickly," she told us, "and headed for the shelter at Portland Square, with Blackie, my Cocker Spaniel." But when they got to the entrance the guards turned them away, saying dogs weren't allowed in! "I couldn't bear to leave Blackie alone," said Lillian, who then returned home with her hound. "We listened all night as the bombs fell. I couldn't believe the news the next morning, when I heard so many people had died in the shelter and realized that Blackie had saved my life!"

Did You Know?
Portland Square is now part of the University campus, and in 2006 some remains from the air-raid shelter passages were rediscovered. Graffiti on the wall of one shelter reads 'A. Davis'. Could it have been written by ten-year-old Arthur?

"YES, WE'D BETTER TAKE COVER, QUICK!"

Not so long ago, the University was spread across the South West, with a College of Art in Exeter, a Teacher Training College by the sea in Exmouth and Seale-Hayne, the farming college, in Newton Abbot. But by 2008 all the colleges had moved to Plymouth to become part of one big campus. Did you know that the University has its very own walk of fame? Most of the campus buildings are named after famous people who have links with the South West.

The Sherwell Centre

The Scott Building

1. Work started on the Sherwell Congregational Church in 1862, so this building is as old as the University! It looks very different today, since having a 'makeover' in 1996. It's now the Sherwell Centre, used for exhibitions, lectures, conferences and concerts.

2. Antarctic explorer, Robert Falcon Scott, died tragically in 1912, when his expedition party ran out of supplies and froze to death. Scott was born in Stoke Damerel, Plymouth, in 1868. He began naval training at the tender age of 13! His jobs included working in the rigging – 35 metres above the ship's deck! It can't have put him off, though, because he later became a Royal Navy Captain. The Scott Building used to be a school, but today it's dedicated to the Arts, from photography to music.

Did You Know?

Antony Jinman, the University's own Explorer in Residence, was inspired by Captain Scott. In 2012 he's leading an expedition to the spot where Scott died 100 years earlier.

6 The plan was to name the Roland Levinsky Building after Sir Joshua Reynolds. But on the stormy New Year's Day of 2007, Professor Levinsky was walking his dog in Wembury when, tragically, he was struck by a falling power cable and died. As he had commissioned the striking new building and been Vice-Chancellor since 2002, the University decided to name it after him. Levinsky was a brilliant scientist, but he also loved the Arts (he even made his own pottery) and wanted the new iconic building to be used for all things arty!

7 Charles Babbage had the idea for the first programmable computer nearly 200 years ago! Today the Babbage Building is positively packed with PCs! Charles spent some of his school days in Totnes where his grandfather, Benjamin Babbage was once the Mayor.

Did you know? Charles Babbage's brain is preserved in two different London museums – one half is in a medical museum and the other is in the world-famous Science Museum!

8 For early birds and night-owls, the Charles Seale-Hayne Library has over 495,000 books on offer – and it's open 24/7! Charles Seale-Hayne was MP for the local town of Ashburton and the first Chairman of Dartmouth and Torbay Railway. When he died, he left money to set up a farming college, which later became part of the University.

9 Biologists, geographers and chemists live in the Davy Building. It takes its name from Penzance-born Sir Humphry Davy. Down in the mines, in 1815, there was a serious problem. Miners were dying because methane gas underground could react with the candles on their helmets, and cause catastrophic explosions. Humphry invented a life-saving lamp, which separated the flame from the gas. Today miner's lamps still follow the same principle.

10 Wait patiently at the Portland Square Building, if you want to become a doctor or dentist, because studying for your degree will take five whole years! To keep you on your toes, you'll have lectures across the South West – on the main Plymouth campus, in Truro and at the John Bull Building (named after the University's first Vice-Chancellor) near Derriford Hospital. The Peninsula College of Medicine and Dentistry is a 21st century addition to the University; in July 2011 it celebrated the graduation of its 500th doctor! And in 2013, its name will get even bigger, when it becomes the Plymouth University Peninsula Schools of Medicine and Dentistry. Phew!

11 Although Engineer John Smeaton was born in Yorkshire, he was actually responsible for Plymouth's best-known landmark – Smeaton's Tower! The lighthouse once stood 14 miles out to sea, and was lit by the flames from 24 candles! After powerful waves damaged the Eddystone rocks that it stood on, the building was transported stone by stone and rebuilt on Plymouth Hoe.

You can study Science and Technology in the Smeaton Building. It even has its own laser laboratory!

Your Country Needs YOU!

During the Second World War, men of different ages had to choose between joining the Army, the Navy and the Royal Air Force (RAF):

- In 1939 men aged between 20 and 21 were recruited.
- Later in 1939 men aged between 18 and 41 joined up to fight.

Merchant seamen weren't expected to fight, but delivering supplies in wartime was fantastically dangerous: of 140,000 merchant seafarers at work during the Second World War, a shocking 32,000 were killed – many torpedoed by German U-boats, or submarines!

With so many men away at war, women took responsibility for lots of important roles – from driving ambulances to making bombs.

In Plymouth, higher education continued as the war rolled on, but the lessons were sometimes a little strange! At Plymouth and Devonport Technical College in 1944, one teacher walked into the biology lab to find that there was no glass in the windows!

Land Girls Get Stuck In

Ever heard of the Land Girls, or The Women's Land Army? Most men in their early twenties were expected to complete six months of military training and then head off to war – so the Land Girls worked the farms in their place. At the start of the Second World War only 30 per cent of the country's food was home grown. However, by 1943, with the help of the Land Army, that amount had risen to 70 per cent!

Seale-Hayne Agricultural College was one of the places where the Land Girls were trained to fight the national food shortage. Many of the girls came from cities and had never seen the countryside, let alone cows, before!

The Land Girls quickly learned skills such as how to milk a cow, and when to pick sprouts – frosty, winter mornings were best, though they ended up with numb thumbs! But the worst lesson of all was how to kill a chicken!

The college merged with Plymouth Polytechnic in 1989, where female students still studied farming, so the Land Girls' legacy lived on.

In this section you'll find out all about the University buildings and the local VIPs who've lent them their names. Each fact links to a number on the map, starting with the oldest on the outside! Keep your camera clicking and see if you can find everything as you go...

Did You Know?

In the 19th century, there was a bone-crushing mill on the s site of Drake's Place Gardens. Sounds grisly, but it was for crushing animal bones to make glue!

 Sculptor, Barbara Hepworth, was one of the best female artists of the 20th century. Her studio in St Ives, Cornwall, where she died accidentally in a fire in 1975, is now a museum. Applications from would-be students are processed in Hepworth House by the University's admissions team.

 Everyone's heard about Sir Francis Drake's discoveries and battles at sea, but in the 16th century Drake also helped improve Plymouth's water supply – by bringing water down to the town from Dartmoor. A reservoir was built near the Plymouth campus, as Plymothians got increasingly thirsty! You may know it as Drake's Reservoir.

 The Reynolds Building was once a bank. It takes its name from Sir Joshua Reynolds – the famous 18th century portrait painter. Born in Plympton in 1723, Reynolds moved to London at 17, where he ended up painting likenesses of all the celebrities of his day! This building houses some of the University's excellent engineers.

Isaac Foot was born in Plymouth in 1880 and was a local politician and solicitor. During the Second World War, he was a security adviser to Prime Minister Winston Churchill's cabinet. He must have been a bookworm too, as he presented Plymouth City Library with around 9,000 books during his lifetime! The **Isaac Foot Building** is like a giant common room for University staff, and students come here to get advice on their finances.

American-born, **Nancy Astor** defeated Isaac Foot in the 1919 elections and went on to serve as a local MP for 26 years. She was Lady Mayoress of Plymouth during the Second World War (her husband, Waldorf Astor, was Mayor) and the first woman ever to take her seat in the Houses of Parliament! **The Nancy Astor Building** is used by trainee nurses and midwives. There's a student gym in here too.

 The **Cookworthy Building** has been the home of Plymouth Business School since 1994. **William Cookworthy** made the first true English porcelain and discovered China clay in Cornwall.

 Isambard Kingdom Brunel was a brave and bold engineer, so **Brunel Laboratories** seems a good place to train engineers of the future. Brunel designed and constructed a network of tunnels and bridges for the Great Western Railway, including the Royal Albert Bridge that crosses the River Tamar from Plymouth to Saltash. Other engineers thought it was impossible to build a bridge there, because the river was 300 metres wide!

It seems right that **Mary Newman Halls** and **Francis Drake Halls** (where some students live) are close together, as Mary married Sir Francis in 1569. Mary was born in Saltash and buried in St Budeaux in 1582, but nobody knows exactly where her grave is – maybe she haunts the halls…!

Cracking Courses: Marine Biology

The Diving and Marine Centre is the only place in the country where you can learn to dive professionally as part of your degree. In fact, the University is home to Europe's largest Marine Institute! The Diving Centre performs over 5000 safely supervised dives per year – and luckily there are no sharks circling below… or are there?

CAN YOU SPOT?

These things aren't marked on our map and you might be surprised to find them on a university campus:

A **Totem Pole** that is over five metres tall and carved from red cedar wood by Canadian artists. **Harry Potter stuck in the wall.** Actually, it isn't really Harry. This sculpture was completed in 1984… Harry Potter wasn't in print until 1997! The **Immersive Vision Theatre** helps astronomers to discover more about the universe. Inside, students are surrounded by screens that transport them to another city, country or planet! **Four large wood carvings** of the elements: Earth, Air, Fire and Water. The **Hope Sculpture** commemorating the Portland Square bombing.

Answers at the back of the book.

ALL THINGS ARTY

That's the end of the history lesson. But what would the students of 1862 think about today's University? Well, they'd be pleased the University still teaches Navigation, alongside lots of other nautical courses – like Ocean Exploration and Maritime Business.

They might be mystified by courses like Computing and Games Development, or 3-D Product Design, and they'd be absolutely amazed by the array of Arts courses on offer.

The Faculty of Arts dates back to 1854, when Exeter School of Art opened its doors to budding artists and actors. Today, students still use paintbrushes and pencils, but some courses also use new creative techniques and technologies! The University's Arts events are often open to everyone, so you could get arty here too. You could even come and watch a movie. But be warned, strange things can happen at the Jill Craigie Cinema...

A Few Who've Dared to be Different

Christian Allen took a different approach to his architecture project on 'Everyday Life', by asking for help from Nancy Bean... his three-legged cat! For a few tins of food, Nancy strapped a camera to her neck and prowled the streets of Plymouth. The cat camera snapped automatically 400 times each day for a whole month, to record a cat's-eye view of the world. Nancy's photos ended up on display in a French gallery, which was just purr-fect!

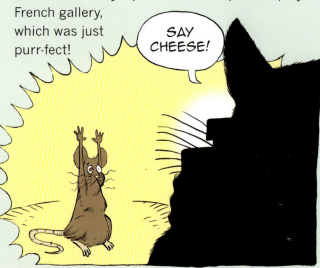

A group of student petrol heads didn't just paint a picture... they painted a car! The Illustration students worked around the clock in 2011 to give the Reliant Scimitar a dazzlingly different design.

When Alexis Kirke decided to create a symphony, he didn't work with an orchestra or ensemble – he used a building instead! He placed light sensors on the Roland Levinsky building – and, when the sun rose, the concert commenced! Starting off slowly, after 30 minutes the composition reached a roaring crescendo of spooky but beautiful music!

Yes, Arts students often work in interesting and unusual ways!

Web Whizzes in Wonderland!

Even IT geeks can get arty sometimes! In 2008 some of the University's computer technicians became part of the production team for Tim Burton's Hollywood blockbuster, *Alice in Wonderland*. Film-makers used the University's high-speed Internet service to beam the latest, top-secret scenes, featuring Johnny Depp and friends, back to the USA!

LOOK WHO'S TOP OF THE GREEN LEAGUE!

What's the University's favourite colour? Green! Plymouth has been a top performer in the Universities' 'People and Planet Green League' for five years! There's all sorts of eco-friendly stuff happening:

Green Building – The Levinsky Building may be covered in recyclable copper, but it's designed and built with more than a hint of 'green' in mind. Among its many eco-features are the tanks in the roof for collecting rainwater that'll flush the building's loos.

Green Screen – Eco-hero Chris Munro got his 'cycle-cinema' idea from Indian villagers who use pedal power to light up their homes! Two trailers attached to his bike stored a projector and sound system. As Chris pedalled, the projector powered up and showed a series of green movies.

Green Science – When the University held its climate change road show, one exhibit was a tiny tornado! It was designed to show locals what the weather might be like in 50 years' time. Full-size twisters can spin at speeds of up to 300 miles per hour and measure up to two miles wide. This one was just one metre high, had the power of a normal vacuum cleaner and was tame enough to touch!

Giant Green Jigsaw – Students and locals puzzled over ways to transform an area of dull, disused land into the attractive City Jigsaw Garden. The garden sits halfway between the Roland Levinsky building and the Drake Circus Shopping Centre and will be used for public events. But why's it called a 'Jigsaw' garden? Well, because parts of it can be lifted and moved to different areas of the city – just like the pieces of a giant jigsaw puzzle!

Cracking Courses: Wildlife Conservation

Want to protect pandas and stop people standing on snails? Well, enthusiastic environmentalists can study green subjects such as Wildlife Conservation. Fieldtrips include watching baboons behave badly.

ROBOTS AND REVELATIONS

Have you ever wondered who makes the amazing discoveries you often hear about on the news? Well, some of them happen at Plymouth University, where super-brainy scientists are always hitting the headlines!

ROY ROCKETS INTO RECORD BOOKS!

2006

Chemistry Professor Roy Lowry entered the UK Fireworks Championships in Plymouth, on a mission to prove that science is exciting! He certainly succeeded, gaining an entry in the Guinness World Book of Records for launching the most firework rockets at the same time – an ear-popping 56,645!

DR MICK SAYS "PLANTS MAKE YOU SICK!"

2009

In the depths of Western Australia, ecologist Dr Mick Hanley discovered that flowers aren't brightly coloured just to attract insects. The colour red also tells some animals: "Back off, this plant is poisonous!" So, if you're an emu, a parrot or a kangaroo, red really does spell danger!

PLANKTON PUSH PARTRIDGE FROM PEAR TREE!

2010

Fish eat it, whales eat it, and if you've ever been swimming in the sea you've probably eaten it too! But did you know that without plankton the ocean would be deserted? Dr Richard Kirby is so potty about plankton, he made up the Twelve Plankton of Christmas!

Three wise men

Ship Simulator

Land Ahoy! The School of Navigation once trained students to sail the seven seas using only a compass and sea-chart. Nowadays students can jump into a state-of-the-art Ship Simulator and learn to sail different ships, from a speedboat to a colossal cruise-liner, without getting wet! The simulator can mimic real-life weather conditions so well, you might even feel a little seasick!

Secrets of the Robot Lab

Bet you wish you could learn more about robots at school! Well, guess what? The Faculty of Science and Technology has its own Robot Laboratory! You can actually take a degree in Robotics, and invent, experiment and play with robots all day long...

Name: Football Bot

Mission: to win the World RoboCup!

Greatest Achievement: part of the University's team which won the World RoboCup from 2003 to 2007!

Name: iCub (aka 'Titch')

Mission: to learn to recognize words and their meanings.

Special Feature: webcam eyes that can recognize colours and objects.

HOW MANY FACTS HAVE WE GOT NOW?

I DON'T KNOW – ICUB'S TAKEN MY CALCULATOR!

PROCESSING, PROCESSING... 145 FACTS. BEST FACTS SO FAR – THE ONES ABOUT ME.

Magnificent Magnification!

Fancy a journey into a whole new world? In the Electron Microscopy Centre you can see what it's like to be little! Three different types of microscope are used to make the minute look massive – from bugs to bacteria!

Who's this creepy critter? It's a beastly bed bug that's actually only three millimetres long! It's been magnified to around 100 times its normal size. These mini-bloodsuckers creep up on us when we're sleeping. They use their sharp snouts to pierce our skin... before feasting on our blood! And without magnificent microscopes, we wouldn't even know!

In fact, some transmission electron microscopes can magnify a sample up to *one and a half million times* its normal size! And that's why these microscopes are so special – they help scientists to find out how deadly diseases can attack the human body!

Cracking Courses: Computing and Games Development

Want to reach the next level? As part of this course you get the chance to work for a computer games company for a whole year!

GRADUATION AND BEYOND

When all the hard work towards their degree is over, students can celebrate! Each year the University holds its graduation ceremonies on Plymouth Hoe.

Around 30,000 students are studying at Plymouth University at any one time. When they graduate, they head off to start all kinds of careers. Some become nurses, doctors, social workers, lawyers, engineers or teachers. But others search out more unusual careers...

FOUR Modern-Day Cadets!

1) With her first-class honours degree in Marine Biology, Tooni Mahto became a daring diver and fearless underwater filmmaker. She's worked as a presenter and expert on the BBC documentary series Oceans and now has over 2,000 dives to her name!

2) Imagine going to work on a speedboat and getting paid to teach the likes of Harrison Ford and Steven Spielberg to kite-surf! Well, Applied Sports Science graduate, Gemma Brill, does just that. She works on billionaire businessman Sir Richard Branson's private Caribbean island!

3) What can you do with a degree in Ocean Science and Meteorology? Become a world-class yachtsman, of course, just like Conrad Humphreys! At the age of 26 he became the youngest skipper to win the round-the-world 'BT Global Challenge'.

4) One student was a sailing success before he even came to the University. When he was only 15, Seb Clover became the world's youngest sailor to cross the Atlantic Ocean single-handed. He studied at the University from 2005.

THREE Tremendous TV Stars!

1) Soap star Pam St Clement, who played 'Pat Butcher' in *Eastenders* for 25 years, wasn't always an actress! Pam trained to be a teacher at Rolle College in Exmouth, which is now part of the University. In 2008, the University awarded her an honorary doctorate in Education.

2) BBC wildlife presenter Monty Halls is a real globetrotter! With his first-class degree in Marine Biology, he travelled right around the world FOUR TIMES! On one expedition in India he discovered a mysterious sunken city that everyone had thought was just a local legend!

3) Michael Underwood is a born entertainer! With a degree in Drama and Performance, he went on to present on CBBC and the 'Entertainment Today' segment of GMTV. He's even appeared in *Dancing on Ice* – we won't mention the bit where he fell over and broke his ankle!

TWO Brilliant Business People!

1) Why not follow in the fashionable footsteps of Business Administration graduate, Rob Drake-Knight? His award-winning clothing brand, Rapanui, makes 'green' garments from natural and organic fabrics, in factories run on wind-power! The brand is named after the people of Easter Island, whose fertile land turned back to rock after they used up all the trees!

2) Can you keep a secret? Well, entrepreneur Dominic List, who studied Design Technology and Business, certainly had to when he went on Channel 4's *The Secret Millionaire*! The programme asks people with pots of money to go undercover, before giving some of their cash to those who work hard for the community.

ONE who changed course completely...

You don't always have to find a job to do with your degree. Andy Cameron studied Politics, but instead of heading for 10 Downing Street – he ended up running a successful Surf School in Polzeath, Cornwall. He could have studied...

Cracking Courses: Marine Sport Science

On this course students study the sea and the stars, sports equipment design and business skills. They sometimes get to ride the waves too!

Oh, and 3,000 Hard-working Staff...

Wendy Purcell left Plymouth University in 1985 with a degree in Biological Sciences. She went on to become a professor but came back to Plymouth 20 years later as the University's first female Vice-Chancellor.

Professor Purcell is in charge of 3,000 staff! That includes cooks, librarians, administrators, lecturers... And of course there are other professors, like geologist, Iain Stewart, who studies earthquakes, tsunamis and volcanoes! As if that's not enough, he also presents BBC documentaries on Geology in his spare time!

PLYMOUTH UNIVERSITY – THE PRESENT, THE FUTURE... AND BEYOND!

There's loads more going on at Plymouth University, and lots more exciting stuff happening any minute...

The ground-breaking Marine Building opens in 2012, with a state-of-the-art wave testing machine inside! The machine will make waves form in different directions and create changing currents in both shallow and deep water. It's all part of the search for environmentally friendly energy!

The Marine Institute has a new research vessel – a catamaran! It's called *Falcon Spirit*, after Captain Robert 'Falcon' Scott! On board is a remote-control diving vehicle, which can capture underwater scenes in high definition at up to one kilometre beneath the surface.

And just in time for the 150th celebrations, in 2012, the University will be awarded a prize by the Queen for its work in marine and maritime teaching and research.

But what will the University be like in 25 years' time? It's impossible to say for sure, but we asked some University VIPs what they thought the future might hold. Here's what they said:

- With e-books and handheld computers, paper may be a thing of the past!

- Marine and ocean science will be even more important. Global warming means rising sea levels – maybe the sea will be closer to the campus. Yikes!

- There will be more courses aimed at finding better ways of coping with climate change.

University of New Plymouth on the Planet Inmula

And in 150 years? Well, we can only dream about that, but maybe...

- doing your degree might be more like playing a computer game; information could be beamed directly into your brain!

- there could be a degree in Intergalactic Tourism.

- the University might be underwater, or even on another planet!

As for what really happens, you'll have to wait and see, but who knows – with life expectancy going up and up – you might still be around in 2162 to see for yourself! One thing's for certain, though, Universities will be needed more than ever in the future to answer the big questions the world is facing: How do we feed the ever-expanding population? How do we handle climate change? Where will we find our energy?

But you'll be answering some big questions of your own in a few years' time. What will you do when you're older? Would you like to go to University? Will *you* be one of Plymouth University's students of the future?